KT-438-645

A YEAR OF FESTIVALS

book is to be returned on or before the

Jewish Festivals

Honor Head

WAYLAND

Explore the world with **Popcorn** - your complete first non-fiction library.

Look out for more titles in the Popcorn range. All books have the same format of simple text and striking images. Text is carefully matched to the pictures to help readers to identify and understand key vocabulary.
www.waylandbooks.co.uk/popcorn

Published in paperback in 2012 by Wayland
Copyright © Wayland 2012
This edition published in 2014

Wayland
Hachette Children's Books
338 Euston Road
London NW1 3BH

Wayland Australia
Level 17/207 Kent Street
Sydney NSW 2000

Produced for Wayland by
White-Thomson Publishing Ltd
www.wtpub.co.uk
+44 (0)843 208 7460

All rights reserved.
Editor: Jean Coppendale
Designer: Amy Sparks
Craft artwork: Malcolm Couch
Subject consultant: Rabbi Rachel Montagu
Series consultant: Kate Ruttle
Design concept: Paul Cherrill

British Library Cataloging in Publication Data
Honor Head
    Jewish festivals -- (A year of festivals)(Popcorn)
    1. Fasts and feasts -- Judaism -- Juvenile literature.
    I. Title II. Series
    296.4'3-dc22

ISBN: 978 0 7502 6971 1

Printed and bound in China

10 9 8 7 6 5

Wayland is a division of Hachette Children's Books,
an Hachette UK company.
www.hachette.co.uk

Picture Credits: Alamy: 12 Nathan Benn; 13 Art Directors & Trip; 16 Israel Images; Chris Fairclough: 6, Front Cover/14; Dreamstime: 10 Paul Cowan; 11, 15 Howard Sandler; 18, 19/1, 20 Lisa Young; Getty Images: 17 Fuse; 21 Steve Allen; Shutterstock: 4, 7/2, 8 Noam Armonn; 5 Lisa Young; 9 Diligent

Contents

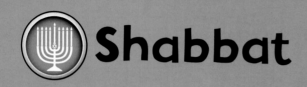# Shabbat

Shabbat begins on Friday evening every week with a special meal. It finishes on Saturday night. It is a time to rest and think of God.

On Friday night, Shabbat begins by lighting candles.

At the end of Shabbat, everyone sniffs sweet spices so that they remember the sweetness of Shabbat during the week.

During Shabbat no one does any work.

At the Shabbat meal, people eat a special bread called challah. This reminds everyone of God's goodness.

# Passover

Passover is when people remember how God brought the Jews out of Egypt, the land where they lived.

Passover takes place in March or April.

During Passover, and other festivals, the Rabbi reads from the Torah, the Jewish holy book.

The Jews had to escape because the king of Egypt wanted to keep them as slaves. They made bread called matzah for the journey.

Matzah is flat, crunchy bread.

Passover meal

At Passover, families get together to have a special meal. Before the meal, everyone reads the Haggadah.

The Haggadah is the story of how the Jews escaped from Egypt.

As part of the meal, the family has
a little taste of some special foods.
Each food reminds them of the good
and bad times of the past.

Horseradish —
a bitter herb

Hard-boiled
egg

Cooked bone,
such as lamb

Parsley

Boiled
potato

Chopped apples
and walnuts

Lettuce

The plate of food is called
the Seder plate.

Rosh Hashanah

Rosh Hashanah takes place in September. It is the Jewish New Year. This is when Jews think about how they have behaved during the past year.

Jews eat slices of apple dipped in honey to wish each other a sweet and happy new year.

Rosh Hashanah lasts for two days.

At this time, Jews try to make up any arguments they have had. They ask God for forgiveness for any bad things they have done.

During Rosh Hashanah, the rabbi blows a ram's horn, called a shofar, to call Jews to turn away from all the wrong things that they have said or done.

Yom Kippur

Ten days after Rosh Hashanah, a festival called Yom Kippur takes place. At Yom Kippur, Jews are not allowed to do anything except pray.

Jews spend the day in the synagogue saying special prayers asking for forgiveness.

During Yom Kippur most Jews
fast. This means they don't
have anything to eat or drink
for a day and night.

During evening prayers, special candles, called yahrzeit
candles, are lit in memory of people who have died.

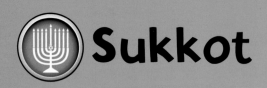

Sukkot

At Sukkot, Jews build a hut outside where they eat their meals for a week. This reminds them of the time when their ancestors had to live in the desert.

Children hang fruit on the walls of the hut.

Sukkot is five days after Yom Kippur.

On the morning of each of the days of Sukkot, Jews wave a lulav which is made of branches and leaves from different trees. They also hold a fruit called a citron.

Jews point the lulav towards
the four points of the compass.
This is to show that
God is everywhere.

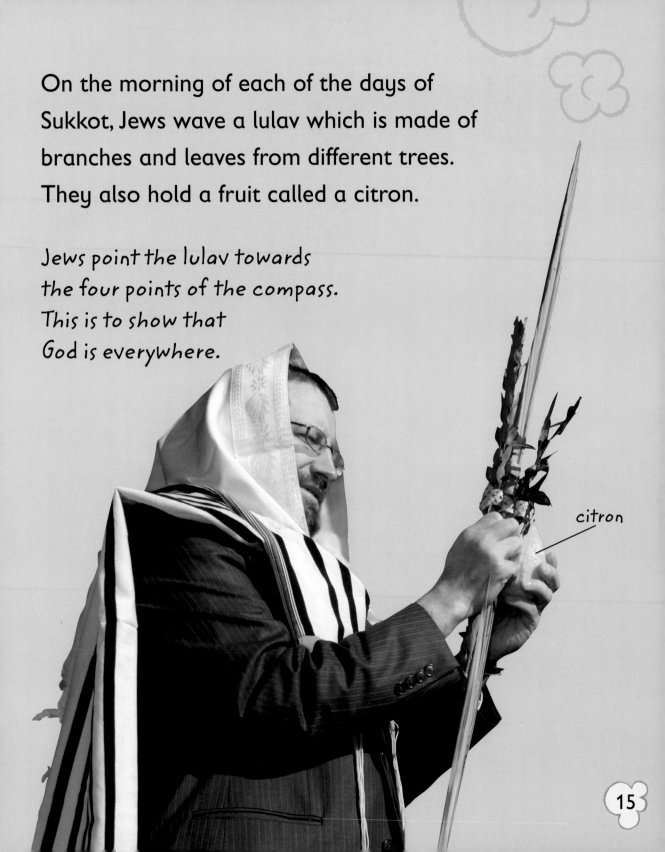

citron

Simchat Torah

This is a very happy festival that
happens the day after Sukkot.
On this day, Jews celebrate
their holy book, the Torah.

In Israel, the Torah is carried through the streets.

At the synagogue, some of the Torah is read out each week. The final part is read on Simchat Torah. Then the Torah is read from the beginning again.

Children are often given sweets and fruit as part of the celebrations.

Hanukkah

At Hanukkah, Jews light a special candlestick called a menorah. This is to remember the miracle of the oil lamp in the temple.

The Hanukkah candlestick has nine candles. The one in the middle is used to light the others.

Hanukkah takes place in December and is also called the Festival of Lights.

Long ago, the Jews did not have enough oil to light the temple lamp. God kept the lamp alight for eight days until more oil came.

Each day during Hanukkah another candle is lit.

Games and food

Special potato pancakes called latkes are made at Hanukkah. They are cooked in oil. This is a reminder of the oil that burned in the lamp in the temple.

Latkes are made from grated potato and onion mixed with flour and egg.

During Hanukkah, Jewish families
play a game called dreidl.
The dreidl is a little spinning top.

To play dreidl you have
to spin the top to win
the chocolate money.

How to make a shofar

Make a shofar as a special gift for Rosh Hashanah.

1. Roll the paper towels to make a cone shape or horn.

2. Cover this with foil and shape it into a shofar.

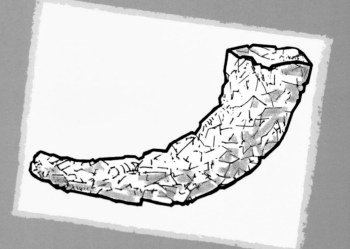

3. Make the paper mache.
Wrap it around the foil shofar.

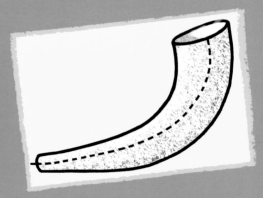

4. Before the paper mache is completely dry, ask an adult to help you to cut the shofar in half from top to bottom.

5. Remove the foil and paper towels. Leave the two shofar halves to dry out completely.

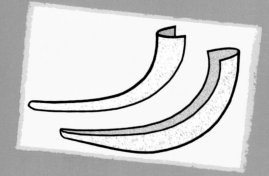

6. Glue the two halves together. When the glue has dried, decorate your shofar with paint or felt tips. Write a message on the side and give it to someone to wish them Happy Rosh Hashanah.

Happy Rosh Hashanah

Glossary

ancestors people from your family who lived a long, long time ago

citron a fruit like a lemon

four points of the compass the four main directions a compass points towards; north, south, east and west.

Haggadah a book that is read aloud on the first night of the Passover. It tells how God helped the Jews to escape from slavery in Egypt.

miracle an amazing thing that happens that no one can explain

prayer a message people send to God

synagogue a special building where Jews go to pray

Rabbi a Jewish leader who knows all about Jewish law, religion and history

temple a building where people go to pray

Index